14 Feb 1998.

Riley

May this make
Learning How to talk to
God easier.

God Bless you

From the Reuters
Mike, Tami, Wyatt
and Taylor.

PRAYERS
FOR BOYS AND GIRLS

Given to

On this date

By

PRECIOUS MOMENTS

PRAYERS
FOR BOYS AND GIRLS

Illustrations by

SAM BUTCHER

Prayers by

DEBBIE BUTCHER WIERSMA

Tommy
NELSON

Thomas Nelson, Inc.
Nashville

Scripture quotations noted CEV are from
THE CONTEMPORARY ENGLISH VERSION. © 1991
by the American Bible Society. Used by permission.
Scripture quotations noted ICB are from
The International Children's Bible, New Century Version,
Copyright © 1986, 1988 by Word Publishing.
Used by permission.

Library of Congress Cataloging-in-Publication Data

Butcher, Samuel J. (Samuel John), 1939-
    Precious moments : Prayers for boys and girls / illustrations by Sam Butcher ;
prayers by Debbie Butcher Wiersma.
    p.   cm.
    Summary: A collection of prayers which speak to common childhood
experiences.
    ISBN 0-8499-1476-0
    1. Children—Prayer-books and devotions—English.   2. Prayers—Juvenile
literature. [1. Prayer books and devotions. 2. Prayers.] I. Wiersma, Debbie
Butcher. II. Title.
BV4870.B88 1997
242'.82—dc21   97-27094
                                                       CIP
                                                       AC

Printed in the United States of America.

97 98 99 00 01 02 03 04 RRD 9 8 7 6 5 4 3 2 1

CONTENTS

NOTE TO PARENTS

Teach your children . . .

and when they are grown

they will still do right.

PROVERBS 22:6 CEV

Jesus said, "Let the little children come unto me...."
In these pages we offer twenty prayers, written
specifically for children. Children use simple, direct,
and honest language when they talk to God. These
prayers, therefore, are simple, direct, and open too.

It is our hope that parents will read these prayers
aloud to their children and that children will be
encouraged to express their thoughts and feelings
freely.

It is also our hope that these prayers will be models
that children can use to create more personal and
meaningful prayers of their own.

THANK YOU, GOD

Thank the Lord

because he is good.

His love continues forever.

1 CHRONICLES 16:34 ICB

FOR MY BODY AND MY MIND

I like how you made me, God.

I'm glad you gave me legs and arms and hands and feet and fingers and toes. I have eyes and ears and a nose and a mouth with lots of teeth.

I have everything I need to enjoy the world you made. I can do all sorts of things with the body you gave me. I can go anywhere I want and do anything I wish.

But the best thing about me is that I have a mind to think and to learn about you.

Thank you, God, for making me as I am.

Amen.

You made me in an amazing
and wonderful way.

Psalm 139:14 icb

FOR MY BEDTIME FRIEND

Thank you, God, for my soft, cuddly bedtime friend. I like to feel his soft, furry ears.

If it's dark in my room, I'm not afraid as long as my friend is there. Sometimes when I'm sad I bury my face in his tummy and cry. He makes me feel better. He's been my friend for so long, I don't remember being without him.

Thank you for giving me a special friend.

Amen.

God…blesses us with
everything we need to enjoy life.

1 Timothy 6:17 cev

FOR BIRDS

Thank you, God, for making birds.

I laugh when I see them flying up and down and turning circles in the air. When birds are way up in the sky, they make me think of angels. The very best thing about birds is their song.

Thank you, God, for the birds that sing to me.

Amen.

God said, "Let…birds
fly in the air above the earth."

GENESIS 1:20 ICB

FOR MY FRIENDS

My friends are very important to me.

They make me laugh when I don't feel happy. They go places with me and play my favorite games. My friends can be trusted to keep all my secrets. When we're together, we always have so much fun.

Thank you for giving me such good friends.

Amen.

I love those who love me.

PROVERBS 8:17 ICB

FOR THE RAIN

Thank you for the rain, God. Sometimes I feel sad when it rains, because I can't go outside to play. Then I think about all of the good things rain does. Rain waters the flowers and grass in my yard. Rain gives the trees a drink. Rain waters the farmers' crops. When I think of all these good things about rain, I'm happy instead of sad. Oh, I almost forgot the very best part about rain—it makes mud puddles for splashing. Thank you for letting it rain, God.

Amen.

He fills the sky with clouds.
He sends rain to the earth.

PSALM 147:8 ICB

FOR MY PET

Thank you for my pet, dear Lord. Some of my friends have dogs or cats. Some have fish or birds. Some even have snakes or lizards for pets. My pet is the perfect pet for me. I can take care of her and love her, and I can tell how much she loves me. When I have the worst kind of day, I come home and see my pet do something funny, and all my bad feelings go away. A smile comes to my face. I want to thank you for my pet.

Amen.

All people and
animals are under your care.

PSALM 36:6 CEV

FOR MY FAMILY

Thank you, God, for my family.

I think I have the best family in the world. Sometimes we have disagreements and sometimes we argue. But I always know my family loves me.

We help each other out with problems, and my family always seems to understand when I'm feeling sad. I've had lots of fun times with my family. As long as I'm with them, I'm happy.

God, I'm glad you decided to give me to this family.

Amen.

It takes wisdom

to have a good family.

PROVERBS 24:3 ICB

I'M SORRY, GOD

You are a

forgiving God.

You are kind and

full of mercy.

NEHEMIAH 9:17 ICB

ABOUT LYING

I told a lie today, God.

It didn't seem like a big lie. It didn't seem like it would hurt to tell one little lie. But it did hurt, God. It hurt me to know that I lied. Even if no one ever finds out, I will always know.

Please help me to tell the truth from now on. If I want to tell a lie, please remind me how awful it will make me feel. I want always to tell the truth so people will always believe what I say.

Please forgive me for lying, God.

Amen.

Don't ever say
things that are not true.

PROVERBS 4:24 ICB

ABOUT CHEATING

Dear God, please forgive me for what I did today.

I cheated on a paper at school, and I feel very bad about it. I didn't know the answer. I didn't want to get a bad grade, so I looked at someone else's answer and wrote it down.

I know that cheating is wrong, but I just didn't think about it. I have to tell the teacher what I did, and I need your help.

Please help me to tell her the truth, and please help me never to cheat again.

Amen.

You notice everything I do.

PSALM 139:3 CEV

ABOUT FIGHTING

I got in a fight today, God.

Even though I said it was all the other boy's fault and he said it was all mine, we were both to blame. Neither one of us had to fight if we hadn't wanted to. We were just so mad!

I don't even like to fight, God. Fighting isn't the right way to settle anything. I would like to think that I'm smart enough to talk to someone about a problem instead of hitting him.

I'm sorry that I hit that boy, God.

Amen.

Don't be a fool and quickly
lose your temper.

PROVERBS 29:11 CEV

ABOUT HURTING SOMEONE'S FEELINGS

I'm sorry about what I did today, God.

I said a very mean thing to my friend, and it hurt her feelings. She looked as if she were going to cry. I wanted to take back what I said, but I was too embarrassed.

Now I feel terrible. I have to tell her how sorry I am, or I'll just feel worse and worse. Please help her to forgive me. And please help me to think before I say something that could make someone feel bad.

In your name, I pray.

Amen.

Careless words stab like a sword.

PROVERBS 12:18 ICB

HELP ME, GOD

God…always helps
in times of trouble.

PSALM 46:1 ICB

WHEN I'M BORED

Dear God, I need your help today.

It's rainy and wet outside, and I can't think of anything to do. I don't want to play with my toys. I don't want to read my books. I don't want to play with my pet.

Please help me think of something fun to do.

Thank you, God.

Amen.

Each day brings its own surprises.

PROVERBS 27:1 CEV

WHEN I'M AFRAID

Please help me not to be afraid, God.

When I go to bed at night, it's so dark. Everything looks different from the way it did during the day. My window looks scary with the streetlight shining through. Dark shadows are all over my room. Everything is so quiet.

It's as if I'm the only one here. I know you're always with me, God, so I don't have anything to be afraid of. But when it's dark and quiet, I get scared anyway.

Please help me remember that you're always right here, God, even on the darkest nights. Thank you.

Amen.

I won't be afraid.

You are with me.

PSALM 23:4 CEV

WHEN SOMEONE ISN'T NICE

A boy at school is a real bully, God.

He teases me and picks on me all the time. Sometimes he scares me. Other times he says mean things. His words hurt me, God. They make me want to cry.

I get a sick feeling in my stomach when I think about him. Sometimes I just want to hit him, but I can't because I think hitting is wrong.

Please help me to find a way to get along with this boy. And, God, if he won't be nice to me, please take extra good care of me.

Amen.

God…protects those

who come to him for safety.

PROVERBS 30:5 ICB

HELP OTHERS, GOD

The Lord…watches over

those who put their

hope in his love.

PSALM 33:18 ICB

FOR CHILDREN WHO ARE HUNGRY

Dear God, some children will go to bed hungry tonight, and I want to pray for them.

Some children's tummies never feel full enough. They don't get the vitamins they need, so they can't grow up to be strong and healthy. Their parents do not have money to buy enough food.

I am very lucky to have all that I have, God, but I'd like to pray for other children. Please help them to have a better life.

Amen.

The LORD blesses everyone who
freely gives food to the poor.

PROVERBS 22:9 CEV

FOR OLDER PEOPLE

Dear God, please take care of the older people in the world.

Old people have had years of experiences, and yet no one seems to want to hear about them. It must be lonely, God. Some old people have children, grandchildren, and even great grandchildren, but they never get to visit them.

I can do something to help. I can bring the old people in my neighborhood cookies or help them get their groceries. But most important of all, I can visit with them and listen to their stories.

Amen.

Always be willing to listen.

JAMES 1:19 ICB

FOR POLICE OFFICERS AND FIREFIGHTERS

I want to pray for the police officers and the firefighters, God.

They put themselves in danger to help people they don't even know. Firefighters will go into a burning building to save a person who might be trapped. Police officers try to keep everyone safe by making them obey the rules and laws.

Please take care of the police officers and firefighters who take such good care of me. Thank you, God.

Amen.

The Lord…gives

protection in times of trouble.

NAHUM 1:7 ICB

FOR PEOPLE
WITHOUT A HOME

God, please help all of the people in the world without a home.

I have a warm, safe place to live in, but some people don't. They live in old, broken buildings. Some of them even live on the streets.

Please help these people to find a real home and a soft bed to sleep on. Thank you, Lord.

Amen.

Do good to people who need help.

PROVERBS 3:27 ICB

FOR MY MOM AND DAD

Dear God, being a parent must be really hard.

You have to work to earn money so you can support our family. You have to keep our home clean and cook our meals. Sometimes by the end of the day, Mom and Dad look tired.

Please take care of them. Thank you, God.

Amen.

Honor your father
and your mother.

Exodus 20:12 ICB